FOSSILS

Pictures from the Past

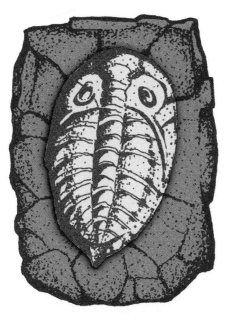

Written by Claire Daniel

STECK-VAUGHN
ELEMENTARY · SECONDARY · ADULT · LIBRARY

A Harcourt Classroom Education Company

www.steck-vaughn.com

Contents

Chapter 1

Long Ago

Imagine that it's a warm day somewhere on planet Earth. The day is much like the day before and the day before that. Rain falls gently on the petals of flowers. Soft breezes blow. Lush green trees are bunched together in a thick forest. Insects buzz and flutter in the gentle wind. The time is about 70 million years ago.

Listen. CRASH! BAM! SMASH! CRUNCH! SCRUNCH! Seven tons (6.3 metric tons) of muscles, bones, and teeth move slowly through the forest in search of food to eat. Here comes *Tyrannosaurus rex* (tye-RAN-uh-SAWR-us rex), sometimes called *T. rex*.

Look beyond the *T. rex*. There are other dinosaurs. You might see another *Tyrannosaurus rex*. This *T. rex* is about the same size and shape as the other one.

Farther away is another dinosaur called *Triceratops* (try-SEHR-uh-tahps). Three horns jut out from its head, protecting it from unfriendly attacks. Imagine that one *T. rex* looking for a meal approaches the *Triceratops*. Perhaps the other *T. rex* wants the same meal. Soon these two mighty hunters fight with each other.

But there is one creature you would not see in this picture of some 70 million years ago. That creature is a human being. The human being did not live at the same time that dinosaurs were roaming Earth.

Dinosaur means "terrible lizard."

If people didn't exist, how do we know so much about dinosaurs? Luckily, some of the plants and animals that lived then tell stories about the past. They give us pictures of what life was like long ago. These stories and pictures are told by the **fossils** the plants and animals left behind.

A fossil is what is left of an animal or a plant that lived long ago. A fossil can be so small that you can see it only under a microscope. Or it can be as large as a 10-foot-long (305 centimeters) dinosaur bone.

Some fossils are quite old. The world's oldest fossils are tiny cells that are 3,500 million years old! "Younger" fossils of fish and ferns have been found. They are between 249 to 408 million years old!

This fish fossil is a picture from the past.

The teeth of an adult *T. rex* were up to 7 inches (18 centimeters) long.

Fossils can be plants or animals. Most fossils are the hard parts of the plants and animals that have been saved, or preserved. These hard parts are bones, teeth, shells, or wood. Fish and other sea creatures, teeth, bones of reptiles, dinosaurs, shells, and tree trunks have all been saved as fossils. Some soft plants and animals such as eggs, insects, leaves, ferns, and spiders have also been saved as fossils.

Human fossils have also been found. That is why **paleontologists**, scientists who study fossils, know how long people have been on Earth. These scientists use the fossils to tell us what life on Earth was like long ago.

Chapter 2

How Fossils Are Made

When a plant or animal dies, it begins to rot away quickly. But the teeth, bones, wood, and shell part of the plant or animal last much longer. These parts can become fossils.

Imagine that a dinosaur dies. After a while, only the **skeleton** is left. Rain falls on the ground and on the skeleton. The water soaks into the ground, carrying **minerals** with it. The water seeps into each dinosaur bone. Then sand or mud covers the bones of the dinosaur. After a time, the water **evaporates**, but the minerals stay. Many years later, the bones turn into a stone or fossil.

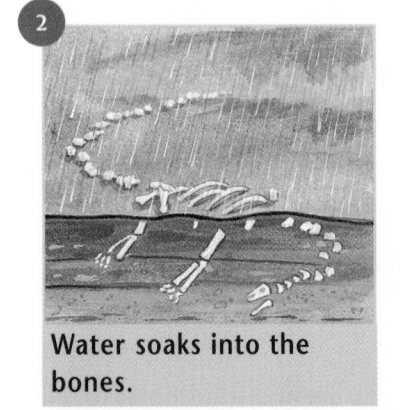

The animal dies.

Water soaks into the bones.

Minerals replace the bone material.

A paleontologist finds the fossils.

Over time the fossil is pushed under the ground. Sometimes a part of the fossil may appear above ground. Scientists searching for fossils may see this and dig it up. Then they have discovered a fossil!

In some parts of the world, bodies of creatures from long ago have been preserved in a yellow stone called **amber**. An animal might have wandered up a pine tree and gotten stuck. The sticky resin, or sap, covered the animal and hardened into amber. The amber stone kept the animal from rotting and disappearing. Insects, spiders, lizards, and even frogs have been found trapped in amber.

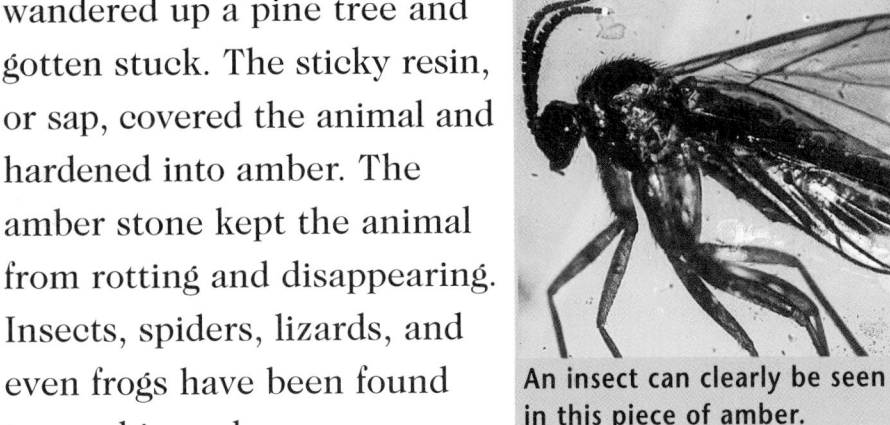

An insect can clearly be seen in this piece of amber.

Other animals, such as woolly **mammoths**, have been preserved in ice from glaciers. Woolly mammoths lived during the time of the Ice Age but disappeared long ago.

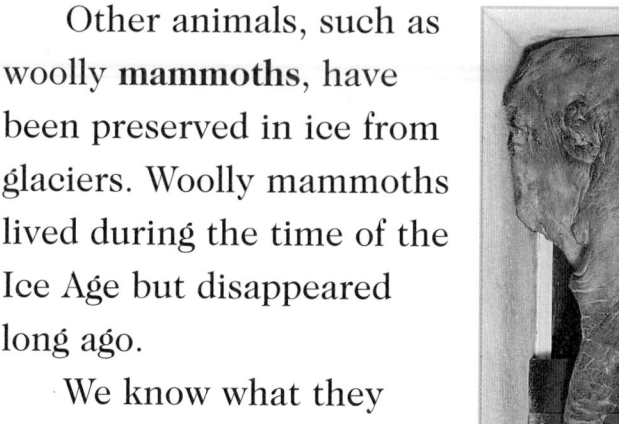

We know what they looked like because we have found their remains in northern Asia and North America. Perhaps the animals fell into large cracks or holes in the ice. The woolly mammoths became trapped and frozen until they were discovered around 12,000 years later!

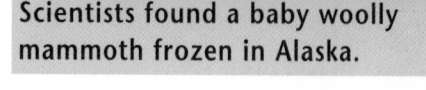
Scientists found a baby woolly mammoth frozen in Alaska.

Plants and insects are less likely to form fossils because both rot away quickly. But a plant or insect might have been buried by sand or mud before it was able to rot. Then it is possible for a fossil to form.

For example, a fern might have fallen to the ground. Perhaps it was quickly buried by mud. Then rain fell, and the minerals filled the air pockets inside the soft leaves of the fern. When the water dried, the minerals stayed. More water came, and more minerals filled the air pockets. Millions of years later, the leaves of the fern hardened into a fossil.

Tree trunks are made into fossils in the same way. **Growth rings** in a tree trunk can tell how old the tree was when it fell. They can also show what the weather was like while the tree was growing. For example, it could tell if there was a lot of rain and how warm it was.

Fossils of trees are called petrified wood.

Fossils of ferns, insects, and flowers have been found all over the world. Plant fossils like these help us know what life was like long ago on Earth.

Chapter 3

Stories Fossils Tell

How do paleontologists figure out what dinosaurs were like? Paleontologists use dinosaur bones to find out.

First, they take the bones to a laboratory. There the scientists lay the bones out in the same order they were found in the ground. Paleontologists compare the bones to other dinosaur bones they have already found. They think about bones of animals that live today. Then the scientists try to figure out what size and shape the dinosaur was. They put the bones together to make a skeleton. They study the skeleton to figure out how the dinosaur stood, how it walked, and what it ate.

Many paleontologists study other kinds of fossils, too. They study fossils of plants and other animals to learn more about life on Earth long ago.

This is a fossil of a poplar leaf thought to be about 25 million years old. The leaf at right is a poplar leaf.

This fossil is of a plant that once grew in the sea. It would attach itself to a hard surface.

This dragonfly, like the one at right, was buried in mud in Germany. Today all that is left is its fossil.

13

Scientists can get an idea of how old a fossil is by testing the rock around it. This is called "dating fossils." Paleontologists can tell what the land was like and what the weather was like on Earth long ago by studying fossils. Scientists can also tell what animals lived on Earth at the same time. The information that scientists find from fossils tells about the past. It helps them determine what may have caused certain animals to become **extinct** at different times.

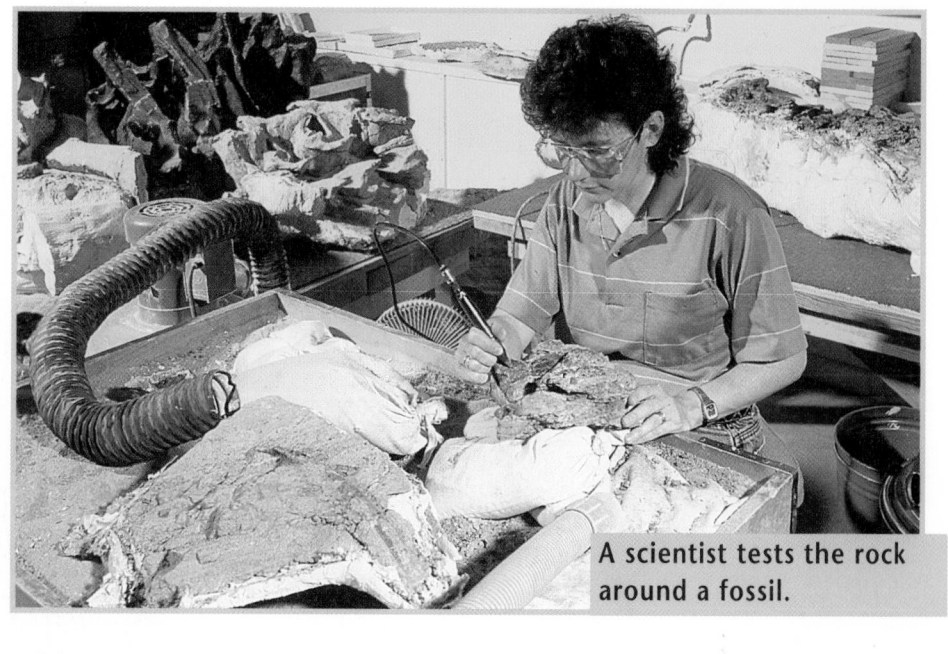

A scientist tests the rock around a fossil.

From studying fossils, scientists believe that the last dinosaur disappeared about 65 million years ago. They know that saber-toothed cats have not roamed the earth for thousands of years. But some animals and plants that scientists find as fossils still exist today.

Plants that still survive and grow today are the monkey-puzzle tree, the ginkgo tree, and the magnolia tree. Cockroaches and dragonflies are the oldest of all insects. They can still be found all over the world. The coelacanth lived more than 350 million years ago. Yet, this fish still swims in the waters between Africa and Madagascar. The tuatara is the only reptile that survived the **Triassic Period**. And it still lives on islands near New Zealand.

A tuatara looks like a modern-day dinosaur.

Chapter 4

Searching for Fossils

Timothy Leland was standing in the Valley of the Moon in Argentina, South America. He had traveled there with a group called *Earthwatch*. Timothy Leland is a writer, not a paleontologist. But he was interested in fossils. So he volunteered to help scientists search for fossils.

The Valley of the Moon is about 250 miles (402 kilometers) from the nearest town. The fossil hunters lived in tents at the campsite. There was no electricity and no running water. At night, it was cool, but during the day it was very hot. A constant wind blew sand everywhere and covered everything with dust.

On the last day of his trip, the temperature reached about 100° F (38° C). Timothy Leland walked slowly in the hot sun. He had been looking for fossils in the valley for two weeks. He had not found very much.

That day Leland hiked across the valley to have a closer look at the cliffs. It was an area that was not thought to have any skeletons of dinosaurs.

Suddenly Timothy Leland stopped and looked at some small pieces of rock sticking up from the sand. The pieces were purplish in color, which usually meant they were dinosaur bones. He looked closer. Four large, sharp teeth looked up at him. Timothy Leland had found the skull of an animal.

Excited scientists ran to the site to take a look. Leland had found not one but two skeletons. But the skeletons were not dinosaur bones. They were the bones of a *Proterochampsa* (pro-TERO-chomp-sah). That is an animal that looked much like the crocodile we know today.

Timothy Leland brushes away sand from fossils.

Few *Proterochampsa* skeletons have been found. The two skeletons that Timothy Leland had discovered were complete. So scientists were eager to study them.

First, the workers dug out as much dirt as possible around the skeletons. They wanted to take the dirt and stone around the skeletons back to the lab where they could work more carefully. So they used shovels, picks, crowbars, and chisels to dig around and below the skeletons.

The workers had to be careful so they would not damage the bones. After a while, they had created a stand for the skeletons.

An *Earthwatch* volunteer looks for fossils in Argentina.

Fossil bones of the *Proterochampsa*

The workers put a special cloth over the bones. They put wet plaster on top of the cloth. The plaster held the bones together so they wouldn't fall apart. Then the workers let the plaster dry. Later, they lifted up the plaster and put it in a truck. The workers took the skeletons back to the laboratory where scientists removed the other dirt and stone from the bones.

The paleontologists will study the bones for many years. They will think about other bones they have found. They will think about crocodiles and other animals they know about that live today. They will put the bones together. Then they will try to figure out how the *Proterochampsas* found in the Valley of the Moon moved and stood.

The Valley of the Moon is famous for fossils from the Triassic Period, a time about 240 million years ago. Today the valley is dry, and few plants and animals live there.

But scientists believe the valley was once covered with ferns and grasses during the Triassic Period. Water was everywhere, and animals could drink from large rivers. Perhaps these rivers overflowed and drowned many animals. Perhaps their bodies were covered by sand. Later their bodies would become fossils.

Today, water and wind have worn away the rock. Many fossils have been uncovered. People like Timothy Leland and scientists travel to the Valley of the Moon. They search for fossils of animals and plants that lived in the Triassic Period.

The Valley of the Moon

Chapter 5

Fossil Discoveries

People have been finding fossils for thousands of years. The name *fossil* means "to dig." Digging is one way some of these early people found fossils. Others found them anywhere rocks were broken and exposed to the air. They might have found them around cliffs and along riverbanks.

In 1822 an important discovery was made. Mary Ann Mantell saw something that looked like a very large tooth lying in the ground. She picked it up and saw that it was hard like a rock. She knew it was a fossil. So she took it to her husband, Gideon Mantell, a doctor.

They studied the tooth and saw it was flat. The rock around the tooth was very old. The tooth was also smooth and worn down, so they knew that the animal had been chewing its food. Was it the tooth of a lizard-like reptile?

21

Gideon Mantell had studied reptiles, and he knew reptiles didn't chew their food. So what was it? He went back to the place where the tooth was found. He dug around and found more teeth and some bones. Other scientists studied the bones with him. They decided they had found the tooth of a very large reptile. They called it the *Iguanodon* (ih-GWAN-uh-dahn).

Soon many other fossils were found. Sir Richard Owen, a scientist, studied these creatures. He knew these reptiles were extinct and no longer lived today. In 1842 he named these creatures *dinosaurs*. In the past 150 years, the remains of hundreds of dinosaurs have been discovered.

The *Iguanodon* was the first known dinosaur.

Sir Richard Owen studied dinosaur fossils.

One of the biggest and fiercest dinosaurs ever discovered is the *T. rex*. Bones from this dinosaur have been found in Canada, Montana, South Dakota, North Dakota, and Wyoming.

For years scientists thought the *T. rex* stood up straight with its tail resting on the ground. They thought it could move quickly. But after studying the skeleton fossils of the *T. rex* more closely, scientists now believe that the *T. rex* walked with its large head forward and its tail sticking out behind it. They also think the *T. rex* could not run fast because it was so heavy.

A *T. rex* skeleton

In 1989 Martin Lockley, a paleontologist, discovered different areas of large dinosaur tracks in Colorado. Lockley named the site the "Dinosaur Freeway." Scientists study these fossil tracks to find out more about how dinosaurs lived.

In 1993 scientists made a surprising dinosaur discovery. They uncovered a complete dinosaur skeleton sitting on a nest of twenty-two eggs.

Bones of a *Triceratops* were discovered in Montana in 1995. These bones had deep bite marks that matched the teeth of a *T. rex*. No doubt, one unlucky *Triceratops* walked into the path of a hungry *T. rex*!

Fossils of dinosaur eggs

In New Mexico in 1996, an eight-year-old boy named Christopher Wolfe found something that was purplish-black and shiny. He picked it up and asked his father, paleontologist Doug Wolfe, if it was rock or bone.

Christopher Wolfe holds the fossil bones he discovered.

Christopher's find was bone. It was part of a horn. He and his father found more than just the horn. They also found jaw parts, a brain case, some teeth, and other fossils. Christopher Wolfe had discovered the fossils of the oldest horned dinosaur ever found. In fact, paleontologists believe the dinosaur is more than 90 million years old.

In China not long ago, many dinosaur eggs were found. Inside the eggs were unhatched baby dinosaurs, called **embryos**. Embryos tell us what kind of dinosaurs laid the eggs.

Fossils of dinosaur tracks are called trace fossils.

Scientists try to answer the question of what really happened to dinosaurs. Some scientists think that the dinosaurs died when a huge volcano erupted, or when acid rain fell all over Earth. Other scientists think that the world became very cold, causing all the plants to die. With no food to eat, the dinosaurs died, too.

Some scientists think that a large meteorite, or stony material from space, fell to Earth, killing the animals and plants that were living there. A huge crater, or hole in the ground, in Mexico is more than 113 miles (182 kilometers) across. It was formed around 65 million years ago. That's about the same time that the dinosaurs disappeared. Did that meteorite kill all the dinosaurs? No one knows for sure. But scientists will continue studying fossils in the hope of finding out.

This crater was made by a meteorite that hit Earth.

Chapter 6

Be a Fossil Hunter

Finding dinosaur bones in your backyard will probably be impossible. But you can collect other fossils.

If you decide to hunt for fossils, you may need to wear a helmet and safety goggles. The helmet protects your head from rock or dirt that might fall. Goggles keep your eyes safe from pebbles you chip off that might spray at your face.

You will also need a magnifying glass, labels, a notebook, a pencil, hammers, brushes, chisels, and a **trowel**. Be sure you ask the landowner if you can search on the land.

Fossils can be found almost anywhere.

If you find a fossil, the first thing to do is to write down in your notebook where you found it. You could also draw a picture of the fossil and the place where you found it. Then use a tool to chip away the rock around the fossil. Use a brush to clear dirt or sand from soft rocks. Try not to damage the fossil.

Clean the fossil with water. Then store it in a box so that it does not get damaged. Label each piece. Then you will know what it is, where you found it, and when you found it.

Digging for fossils is a lot of hard work. Years can pass before an important fossil is found. Still, paleontologists continue to find new exciting fossils. Perhaps you'll discover a fossil, too. Each discovery is worth the wait!

Many rocks contain fossils.

If you do not want to dig for fossils, you can find fossils of plants and animals at a museum. By looking at the fossil exhibits, you can see for yourself what life was like millions of years ago.

Each fossil tells a story and gives a picture of one living thing. With each fossil that is discovered, we have one more piece of a giant puzzle that will tell the history of Earth. Scientists believe that there are many stories waiting to be told of a world long ago.

Fossil exhibits show how large dinosaurs looked.

Glossary

amber a stone made from the resin of pine trees

embryo a young animal before it has been born

evaporate to change from a liquid to a gas

extinct no longer alive

fossil remains preserved in the earth's crust

growth rings rings in a tree trunk that give the tree's age

Iguanodon the first-known dinosaur

mammoth an extinct elephant that once lived in the Northern Hemisphere

mineral a hard substance that is not made of plants or animals

paleontologist a scientist who studies fossils

Proterochampsa a crocodile-like animal

skeleton bones that hold together the body of an animal

Triassic Period a time about 240 million years ago

Triceratops a plant-eating dinosaur

trowel a tool with a flat blade used for digging

Tyrannosaurus rex; **or** *T. rex* a meat-eating dinosaur

Index